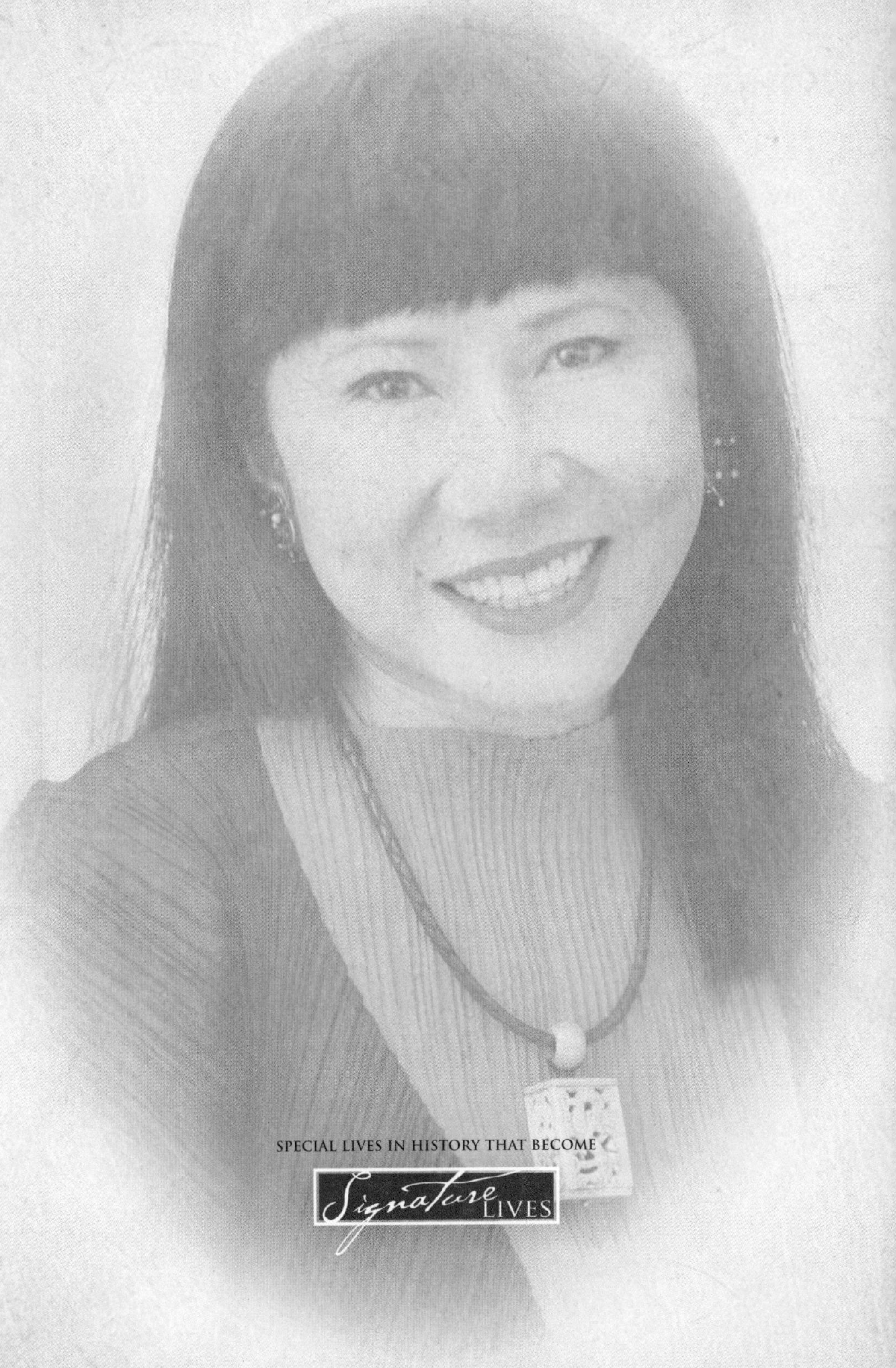

SPECIAL LIVES IN HISTORY THAT BECOME

Signature LIVES

# AMY
# TAN

## AUTHOR AND STORYTELLER

# AMY
# TAN
## *AUTHOR AND STORYTELLER*

by Natalie M. Rosinsky

Content Adviser: Leslie Bow, Ph.D.,
Director, Asian American Studies Program,
University of Wisconsin–Madison

Reading Adviser: Katie Van Sluys, Ph.D.,
School of Education,
DePaul University

COMPASS POINT BOOKS  MINNEAPOLIS, MINNESOTA

Compass Point Books
3109 West 50th Street, #115
Minneapolis, MN 55410

Visit Compass Point Books on the Internet at *www.compasspointbooks.com*
or e-mail your request to *custserv@compasspointbooks.com*

Managing Editor: Catherine Neitge
Page Production: Blue Tricycle
Photo Researchers: Marcie C. Spence and Svetlana Zhurkin
Cartographer: XNR Productions, Inc.
Library Consultant: Kathleen Baxter

Art Director: Jaime Martens
Creative Director: Keith Griffin
Editorial Director: Carol Jones

**Library of Congress Cataloging-in-Publication Data**
Rosinsky, Natalie M. (Natalie Myra)
    Amy Tan : author and storyteller / by Natalie M. Rosinsky.
        p. cm.—(Signature lives)
    Includes bibliographical references and index.
    ISBN-13: 978-0-7565-1876-9 (hardcover)
    ISBN-10: 0-7565-1876-8 (hardcover)
    ISBN-13: 978-0-7565-1982-7 (paperback)
    ISBN-10: 0-7565-1982-9 (paperback)
1. Tan, Amy. 2. Novelists, American—20th century—Biography.
3. Chinese Americans—Biography. I. Title. II. Series.
PS3570.A48Z74 2006
813'.54—dc22  [B]            2006002994

*Signature Lives*

# MODERN AMERICA

Starting in the late 19th century, advancements in all areas of human activity transformed the world into a new and modern place. Inventions prompted rapid shifts in lifestyle, and scientific discoveries began to alter the way humanity viewed itself. Beginning with World War I, warfare took place on a global scale, and ideas such as nationalism and communism showed that countries were taking a larger view of their place in the world. The combination of all these changes continues to produce what we know as the modern world.

Amy Tan

# Table of Contents

# *Chapter*
# 1  A FAMOUS STORYTELLER

❦❧

It was January 2001. A colorful surprise greeted families arriving at San Francisco's Symphony Hall for a special performance. Outside the doors, dancers in huge lion costumes shook their fierce, white and red heads. Later, boys and girls watched wide-eyed as these lions roared onto the stage. Their dance was a traditional part of celebrating the Chinese New Year. Families from many backgrounds had also come to hear music and a story in honor of this upcoming holiday. The storyteller was Amy Tan. On this day, the famous writer was going to read from her picture book titled *The Chinese Siamese Cat*. This featured book was so successful that a new television series was being made about it.

Elegantly dressed in black and gold, Tan perched

*A colorful lion dance is part of traditional Chinese New Year festivities in San Francisco.*

on a tall stool as she read the tale of a mischievous kitten named Sagwa. Her words described how long ago in China, Sagwa helped a foolish magistrate to finally make a wise decision. The magistrate wrote an order to outlaw play and music, but Sagwa's inky tail blotted out part of this order. Instead, the words made everyone, even the magistrate, happy by declaring that "people must sing."

While the audience listened to Tan, they watched the vivid illustrations by artist Gretchen Schields projected onto a screen behind the San Francisco Symphony. They enjoyed the orchestra's sound effects, too. Speaking about a similar performance

*Amy Tan read at the annual Chinese New Year celebration concert of the San Francisco Symphony.*

in Los Angeles, Tan remarked that "children especially seemed delighted upon hearing the sounds violins made to interpret cat yowls."

While some children might have known Amy Tan, it was more likely that adults knew her because of her award-winning novels. Readers connect with Tan's novels and picture books because they touch on universal emotions and experiences while introducing readers to Chinese culture. This blend of ideas makes her works so popular that, as one literature expert notes, Amy Tan's books appear on "the shelves of airport newsstands as well as university bookstores."

Amy Tan was introduced to readers in 1989 with her first novel, *The Joy Luck Club*. It held a place on *The New York Times'* bestseller list for hardcover books for a remarkable 34 weeks. Later, in paperback, it was again a best seller for nine more months. This novel about relationships between mothers and daughters appealed

*Chinese New Year is a winter holiday lasting 15 days. Its exact date changes each year, since the Chinese calendar is based on movements of the moon as well as the sun. People have been celebrating Chinese New Year for more than 4,000 years. Farmers started the holiday to note the end of winter and the beginning of spring. During this holiday, families honor their ancestors and the gods, eat special foods thought to bring good luck, and gather in homes decorated especially for the new year. Some people try to settle all debts during this time. The dragon dance is an ancient Chinese tradition. It has become an important part of New Year's celebrations held in the United States by Chinese-Americans.*

to different ages. While *The Joy Luck Club* was nominated for many adult awards, it also was included on the American Library Association Best Books for Young Adults list. It became the literature selection for the 1992–1993 Academic Decathlon, a yearly national competition for high school students. *The Joy Luck Club* was translated into 36 languages and made into a movie.

Tan has since written four other successful novels, as well as another picture book titled *The Moon Lady,* each of which continues to move and delight readers. *The Kitchen God's Wife, The Hundred Secret Senses, The Bonesetter's Daughter,* and *Saving Fish from Drowning* have all been eagerly greeted by fans.

In spring 2005, Tan won the Common Wealth Award for Literature. This award honors her for all her works and for her worldwide contribution to literature. Each year, individuals receive Common Wealth Awards for outstanding, worldwide achievement in such areas as the arts, science, or public service. Past winners of the literature award include Toni Morrison, Joyce Carol Oates, and Mexican author Carlos Fuentes.

A collection of Tan's essays, *The Opposite of Fate: A Book of Musings,* helps readers understand how this writer transforms events in her life and own family's history into finely crafted and entertaining fiction. This collection gives a closer look into the

*Amy Tan's collection of essays helps her readers better understand the author and her work. The paperback edition of the essay collection is titled* The Opposite of Fate: Memories of a Writing Life.

heart and mind of a young girl who never imagined she would be this successful—or that she would achieve success at all by writing fiction.

The essays in *The Opposite of Fate* tell readers about the problems Tan faced and show how she slowly learned to be proud to be Chinese-American. As a girl, Amy Tan wanted to escape rather than share her Chinese heritage. And she found pain as well as pleasure in her stormy and trouble-filled family life. ಖ

# 2 FROM CHINA TO AMERICA

*Chapter*

❧❧❧

Chinese immigrants Yuehhan Tan and Du Ching Tan, who went by the names John and Daisy, had great hopes for their new life in the United States. When their daughter was born in Oakland, California, on February 19, 1952, they named her An-mei Ruth Tan. In Chinese, An-mei means "blessing from America." An-Mei became known as Amy. She also had an older brother, Peter, born in the United States in 1950, and a younger brother, John, born in 1954.

But her parents' experiences in China cast a dark shadow on Amy's childhood. When John Tan, an electrical engineer, immigrated to the United States in 1947, Daisy did not accompany him. She was still married to her first husband, a brutal, abusive man. His handsome appearance and smooth manners had

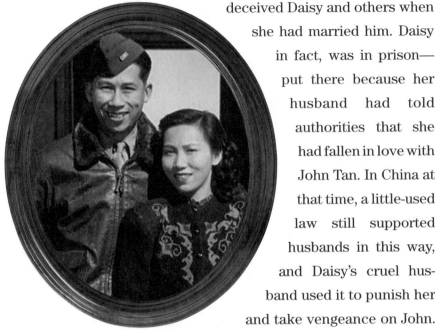

*Amy Tan's parents, John and Daisy, in Tientsin (Tianjin), China, in 1945, before they came to America*

deceived Daisy and others when she had married him. Daisy in fact, was in prison— put there because her husband had told authorities that she had fallen in love with John Tan. In China at that time, a little-used law still supported husbands in this way, and Daisy's cruel husband used it to punish her and take vengeance on John. Daisy and John had first met during World War II, when John was an army translator, and her husband was a Nationalist army pilot.

In the United States, John Tan's distress at this situation was one reason he decided to become a Baptist minister. He continued legal battles to free Daisy from prison and her marriage. After nearly two years in jail, Daisy was able to get a divorce and immigrate to the United States in 1949. She and John Tan immediately married. Daisy, however, could not escape the fears and grief she had lived through in China. Besides the heartaches caused by a bad marriage and harsh laws, Daisy had also suffered the hardships of war.

Throughout the 1930s and 1940s, conflicts raged within China. These included a civil war between Nationalist and Communist Chinese forces, and attacks by the invading Japanese army. Daisy had seen hunger, death, and destruction for many years. Widespread bloodshed did not stop until 1949, when the Communists won the civil war and took control of the government. Many Chinese people who feared the Communists tried to emigrate from China that year.

Most of all, though, Daisy Tan suffered the effects of laws that had forced her to leave three daughters from her first marriage back in China. In addition, Chinese traditions that were rooted in the views of the philosopher Confucius gave all rights over children to their fathers, not their mothers.

Daisy Tan's life in China had left her fearful—both for herself and her new family. She worried about actual and possible dangers. Each time these fears grew too strong, she unreasonably sought safety by moving into a new home. Daisy was determined not to lose this family as she had in China. She fearfully sought to outrun danger, as she had during wartime, by physically moving away from places where she felt threatened. According to Amy Tan, throughout her childhood her family moved every six to 12 months. As a result, she and her brothers frequently had to change schools. By the time Amy finished elementary school, she had been the uncomfortable "new kid" at five different schools. Being Chinese-American in mainly white classrooms made Amy feel even more out-of-place in each new situation.

Daisy expected her children to obey their parents, and her hard life and fears sometimes led her to say harsh things. Amy Tan recalls that, when she was 6, her mother took her to the funeral of a neighborhood playmate. As they looked at the dead little girl in her casket, Daisy in her immigrant English whispered, "This what happen you don't listen to mother." Daisy often used death as a threat with her family, saying she would kill herself when her children disobeyed her or something else had gone wrong. Sometimes, she threatened instead to leave them

*The Tan family in 1952, the day after Amy was born: Peter, John, Daisy, and Amy. Another child, John, was born in 1954.*

and return to China. Tan later wrote with sad humor that these words made her "think that China, like death, was an unpleasant place to go."

One time, her mother's behavior even led young Amy to believe that suicide was an appropriate way to act out her own anger. Six-year-old Amy had seen her mother try to cut her wrists, so when the child was sent unwillingly to bed, she tried to cut her own arm with a butter knife. Fortunately, this dull blade did no real harm. Once Amy realized that even a dull knife "across one's skin actually hurt," she never again attempted suicide.

Young Amy did see that her parents had friends and support from other Chinese-Americans they knew. These included the women her mother met with regularly to play mah-jongg, a Chinese game of skill and chance. They often included members of the different Chinese-Baptist churches that her minister father led. But the effects of Daisy's odd actions and personality outweighed any sense of community for Amy. She was not aware that her experiences as a

*Chinese-Americans are a minority group within the United States. According to the 2000 census, there are approximately 2.4 million Chinese-Americans living in the United States. They form about 1 percent of the country's total population. When Amy Tan was growing up, California already had one of the largest state populations of Chinese-American citizens. By 2000, more than 1 million Chinese-Americans lived there. Today, about 20 percent of the San Francisco area's population is Chinese-American.*

Chinese-American would later become sources of pride, strength, and success. For now, she felt her background to be more harmful than helpful.

Amy's facial features were different from most of the American movie and TV stars she admired. Young Amy once tried to narrow her nose by putting a clothespin on it. At each new school, she was the student whose lunch box contained strange Chinese foods instead of the typical American lunch of sandwiches. Food and physical features weren't the only ways that Amy felt different and distanced from others. She felt even worse when she was the poor ballplayer always picked last for teams during gym.

Amy also knew that her immigrant parents' views about education were much stronger than most of her classmates' parents. As Amy later recalled, "In our family, 'fun' was a bad *f*-word, and its [opposite] was 'hard,' as in hard work. Things that were hard led to worthwhile results; things that were fun did not." She remembers that throughout her childhood, her family took only two brief vacations to Disneyland and Knott's Berry Farm. Instead of going to camp in the summertime, Amy spent her days in Bible classes or summer school, where she "planted sweet peas in milk cartons, or made maps of South America of dried kidney beans, split peas, and lentils."

Amy was bright and did not need summer school to make up work. But her parents insisted that she

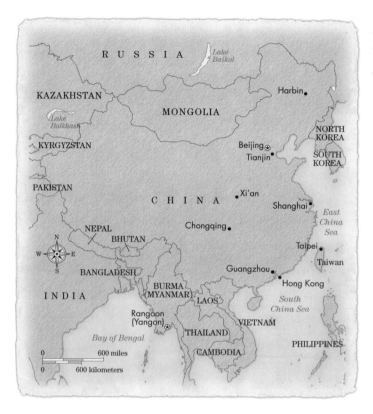

*Amy Tan's parents left China for America after World War II.*

take advantage of free education in the summer. Each good grade that Amy brought home only convinced her parents that she should study more to be a success. Daisy was convinced that, with enough effort, Amy could become both a medical doctor and a concert pianist. Amy, her mother believed, had just as much talent as any musical prodigy they watched on TV. Yet neither parent supported Amy's interest in drawing as a possible career.

Despite John Tan's high expectations for his daughter, he had a tender side, too. Amy fondly recalled sitting on his lap while he read her stories each day. After she learned to read herself, her own favorites included fairy tales and Bible stories. She saw similarities in these accounts, where people's lives changed dramatically through magic or miracles. Sometimes Amy wished that she, too, could magically change her own life.

At age 8, Amy was reading a book a day. She also published her first written work. Amy loved making regular visits to the library. When her local library shut down because the old building was no longer safe, Amy entered an essay contest held as a fund-raiser for a new building. Her essay, titled "What the Library Means to Me," was one of two winners in the elementary school category and was published in a local newspaper, the Santa Rosa *Press Democrat*.

In this brief piece, the third-grader wrote that "the many things I learn seem to turn on a light in the little room in my mind." She went on to explain: "My father takes me to the library every two weeks, and I check five or six books each time. These books seem to open many windows in my little room. I can see many wonderful things outside. I always look forward to go to the library."

At the conclusion of this essay, Amy informed readers that she had given 18 cents to the fund and signed up to be a member of the fund-raising group. Perhaps listening to her father preach sermons in

*An 8-year-old Amy Tan was congratulated for her award-winning essay.*

which he asked church members for donations to charity inspired Amy's words here.

Amy's picture appeared in the Santa Rosa paper. She also won a small radio for her winning essay. The young writer would need these good memories, along with all the "windows" that reading offered her, in the coming years. As she became a teenager, Amy Tan discovered that the problems with her parents and her mother's hurtful remarks—which she later called "the splinters from my childhood"—only became deeper and more painful with time. She also suffered wounds she never expected. ♋

# 3 GROWTH AND GRIEF

❦

When Amy was 10, she learned about her mother's first marriage. She was shocked to discover that—instead of being the middle child of three—she was actually the seventh of eight children. In addition to the three daughters still living in China, Daisy had also given birth there to another daughter and a son. The girl had died soon after birth, while the boy died at age 2 or 3. Amy did not ask for further details. Her life was already complicated because of Daisy's ongoing fears.

To reassure Daisy, Amy's family continued its frequent moves. By the time Amy graduated from high school, she had attended 11 different schools. With each move, Amy quietly watched her new classmates to figure out how to fit in to her surroundings. It was hard to blend in. She did not want to stand out by

*As an adult, Amy Tan embraced the Chinese heritage that had made her uncomfortable in her youth.*

*Amy Tan at age 12 with her cat Fufu in a self-described "glam shot."*

seeming too smart to other kids who might then reject her. Yet she still had to make a good impression on her teachers. Amy later wrote, "I understood that I had to be a chameleon to survive." The growing girl felt only partly successful in this goal.

Amy continued to earn good grades. Even though she already had a published essay to her credit, the young teen got higher scores on math and science tests than she did on English exams. Her parents therefore continued to urge her to study even harder to become a doctor. Amy recalls with sad humor that her parents believed visiting a nearby college campus to be "a form of entertainment" for the whole family. She felt set apart from her classmates because of her parents' intense emphasis on high grades and strict rules about after-school activities. In Amy's words, the Tans insisted on "no boys, no pizza, and of course, no rock 'n' roll."

In part, these rules stemmed from John Tan's beliefs and position as a Baptist minister. Baptists traditionally frowned on dancing and related activities. Instead of having fun at the beach, Amy went there to invite classmates to summer Bible classes. Daisy Tan's traditional Chinese view that girls should behave modestly also limited Amy's after-school activities. Some of Daisy's traditional Chinese ideas, however, were very different than those of Christianity.

In China, many people traditionally believed in ghosts. The spirits could be friendly or they might cause harm. Daisy thought that one of Amy's special talents was an ability to communicate with such spirits. She often asked her daughter to seek advice from the spirit world—about everyday choices and even about such important decisions as investing money. To keep her mother happy, Amy would pretend to communicate with ghosts. Sometimes, the teen tried to get around

*There are many Chinese folktales about ghosts. Spirits supposedly return either to haunt people who harmed them or to help their loved ones. Ghosts are part of traditional Chinese religions. In ancient China, people believed that different spirits inhabited all parts of Earth. Angering a spirit or keeping it happy supposedly affected someone's luck.*

family rules by saying a friendly spirit approved of her going out.

Amy also had to write letters and make business phone calls for Daisy, who was frustrated by her limited English. Sometimes, Daisy even demanded that Amy pretend to be "Mrs. Tan" when phoning for better service or refunds. Amy disliked helping her mother in these ways. It made her feel even more like an outsider among people her age. Most American teens did not perform such tasks for their parents. They did not have to deal with a mother's rage and violent threats if a chore was not completed quickly and well. As her children grew, Daisy's moods continued to swing between love and anger with frightening swiftness.

Amy was hurt by some of Daisy's comments. Amy once asked if she would be considered attractive in China, and her mother replied, "To Chinese person, you are not beautiful. You plain." Amy did not understand that, with this remark, Daisy was trying to reassure herself about her daughter's future happiness. Daisy and other women in her family had suffered because their beauty brought unwanted attention from brutal men.

As a teen, Amy disliked not only her features but her body as well. She thought of herself as unattractive. Amy's shame and discomfort with being so different because of her Chinese heritage reached

new lows with her first high school crush.

When she was 14, Amy fell in love with a white minister's son. She was terrified to learn her parents had invited this minister and his family to Christmas Eve dinner. How would they react to Chinese food and customs? Each detail of the evening was painfully unforgettable. Instead of making the more typical roast turkey and potatoes, Amy's mother was "pulling black veins out of the backs of fleshy prawns" and preparing a whole cod, "with bulging fish eyes that pleaded not to be thrown into a pan of

*John Tan photographed Daisy in China in 1945. Her hard life there had shaped her emotional outlook in ways that her young daughter did not understand.*

hot oil." During dinner, Amy's worst fears seemed to come true.

While their guests waited to be served, Amy's family followed Chinese custom and used their chopsticks to reach into the food platters. Amy felt herself "want to disappear" when her father used his own chopsticks to poke under a fish eye and then offer her a favorite, the "tender fish cheek." The guests ate quietly while Amy's father again followed Chinese customs and loudly belched to show how good the food was. After John Tan explained this custom to their obviously surprised guests, the minister politely managed a small burp himself. His son controlled his laughter at this, but embarrassed Amy could not speak for the rest of the night.

Daisy Tan understood more about her teenager than young Amy realized. Late that night, Daisy wisely said to her: "You want to be same like American girls on the outside. … But inside, you must always be Chinese. You must be proud you different. You only shame is be ashame." Yet it would be years before Amy was mature enough to accept this advice and embrace her Chinese-American identity.

That night, Amy was comforted by the early Christmas gift her mother handed her as they spoke—a new skirt in the latest American fashion. Only years later would Amy also appreciate the fact that all the Chinese foods prepared that night were her favorites. They were another, less obvious gift from her mother.

Amy continued to try to be a typical California teenager. In high school now, she worked part time as a school telephone operator. She tried to be elected secretary of one student government. Yet two unexpected tragedies soon set her apart from most girls her age.

In 1967, doctors discovered that John Tan had a brain tumor. Just months later, Amy's brother Peter also became seriously ill with a brain tumor. Amy later wrote about her feelings as a teenager, watching helplessly during the next year as she saw her "father and brother waste away to skeletons." Amy's father continued to pray and hope for his son's recovery as he himself grew weaker. Nonetheless, 16-year-old Peter's health failed rapidly, and he died in 1967. Seven months later, in 1968, John Tan also died.

Some of Daisy Tan's worst fears about unseen dangers and losing family had come true. Daisy's efforts to deal with this double loss and keep the rest of her family safe soon put an ocean between Amy and the life she had known. ❧

> *Catholic missionaries first traveled to China in the 13th century. Protestant missionaries journeyed there in the 19th century. Amy Tan's father, John, was the son of a Chinese man educated and converted by Christian missionaries. Hugh Tan learned to read and write English before he read Chinese. He became a Presbyterian minister himself. John Tan's 11 brothers and sisters all worked to spread Christianity.*

# 4 CHANGE AND REBELLION

∾◦×◦∾

Along with her own grief, Amy had to deal with new burdens that Daisy placed upon her. There were thank-you notes to write to friends for hospital visits, for attending both funerals, and for making memorial donations. Amy later said it was "torture to write those letters." She kept all of her feelings bottled up inside. Sometimes, Daisy would lash out at her dry-eyed daughter, asking, "What's wrong with you, you don't cry?" What upset Amy the most, though, was how her mother now tried to keep further harm from coming to her family.

While John Tan lived, his Baptist faith and Daisy's Chinese belief in fate influenced by spirits had been the "two pillars of beliefs" in Amy's home. Now, convinced that her family must be cursed to

*The city of Montreux, Switzerland, where Amy Tan would attend school, lies on the shores of Lake Geneva.*

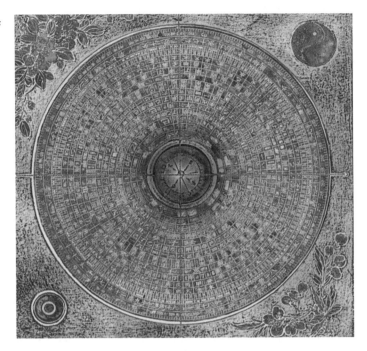

*A special chart is used to arrange a home according to the principles of feng shui.*

have such bad luck, Daisy Tan searched for safety in traditional Chinese practices. She prayed to a picture of her own dead mother. She hired someone to arrange their home according to the principles of feng shui.

Not satisfied with these efforts, Daisy demanded that Amy contact the spirit world, as she supposedly had before, with a Ouija board. Spirits are said to move the pointer on this American message board labeled with letters, numbers, and the words *yes* and *no*. Amy found it heartbreaking to hear her mother ask her dead husband and son, "Do you still love me? Do you miss me?" During these times, the teenager sometimes wondered if the hoped-for spirits might actually be in the room with them.

Daisy also still believed in moving away from possible dangers. Since their home had seen such terrible losses, it now made a strange kind of sense to move very far away. Amy recalls her mother cleaning their kitchen and suddenly looking at a can of Old Dutch cleanser as though it were "a crystal ball." Daisy then announced, "Holland … Holland is clean. We moving to Holland." With those few words, Daisy began a plan that within months uprooted her family.

She sold their house, furniture, and car. She then booked passage for herself, Amy, and young John on a ship sailing to the Netherlands. For several weeks after they arrived, Daisy moved her family from one small city to another. No place seemed suitable, so Daisy took her family by train to Germany. They stayed with an old friend of John Tan's, a U.S. Army chaplain stationed there. Daisy, though, was not satisfied with

> *Feng shui is an ancient Chinese system for designing buildings and gardens. Supposedly, places designed using feng shui are in harmony with nature. People living or spending time in such well-designed environments are said to have a better chance of being happy, healthy, and lucky. In Chinese, feng shui means "wind and water." Experts in feng shui believe in an unseen energy in wind, water, and other natural things. They arrange places and objects in ways that supposedly permit this energy to flow freely yet gently. They also select materials and colors to keep in balance the five natural elements—earth, metal, wood, water, and fire.*

the nearby international school Amy attended, so she again uprooted the family. She bought a small car, packed a handbook that listed private schools in Switzerland, and set off without further planning to check these out. Amy, still trying to get through high school, thought all these moves were crazy, but she went along with Daisy's plans.

The resort community of Montreux, Switzerland, met Daisy's requirements. Many small, older, well-maintained houses lined its cobblestone streets. Daisy found a clean, affordable house she could

*The Alps tower over Lake Geneva near Montreux, Switzerland.*

rent. Most important, the Institut Monte Rosa Internationale was nearby. Daisy believed that the small classes and expert teachers at the school were worth its high cost. Surprisingly, she was not even upset that the school taught the risky sport of skiing on the mountains nearby. Daisy did not know that attending this school would change Amy's behavior.

In the United States, Amy had sometimes tried to bend family rules, but she mainly obeyed them. Now, Amy began to rebel. Her new Swiss school was filled with teenagers from rich families from several different countries. They sometimes got into mischief with the money their families gave them. But what was significant for Amy was that these students and other local young people thought Amy's Chinese features were attractive. They appreciated her dark, waist-length hair. As Amy later recalled, "At last, I was a popular sex object. Life had begun!"

The teenager smoked and snuck out of classes to meet her first real boyfriend, a German man named Franz. Daisy was horrified when she finally met this 24-year-old, who had run away from the German army and now spent most days lounging in coffee shops. Even Amy's younger brother thought that frizzy-haired, casual Franz seemed strange. Daisy and Amy began to have bitter arguments about Amy's continuing to see this young man. These fights led to Amy's saying what she recalls painfully as "the most hateful words I have ever said to another human being. … They rose from the storm in my chest and I let them fall in a fury of hailstones: 'I hate you. I wish I were dead.'"

Sometimes, Daisy's response was a cold silence that lasted for days. At other times, she too spoke with bitter heat. Once she even told Amy, "I wish you the one die! Not Peter, not Daddy." Amy sometimes wondered if the daughters her mother truly loved were the ones she had left in China. These doubts led Amy to further disobey her mother. A worried Daisy renewed her habit of making death threats.

*The Institut Monte Rosa was founded in 1874.*

Amy vividly remembered one episode in which these threats became physical.

After saying she would rather kill herself than see Amy ruin her life with this boyfriend, Daisy announced, "I rather kill you! I rather see you die!" She ran out of their shared bedroom to the kitchen. Daisy then returned with a large knife, pushed Amy against a wall, and held the knife to her throat. Rage gave this small woman strength. Daisy did not move for several minutes, until Amy got past her disbelief and began to cry frightened tears.

Amy planned to run away from home with her boyfriend, but she began to have doubts about him. She was angry but also relieved when a detective hired by her mother discovered that Franz illegally sold drugs. Besides deserting the German army, he had also escaped from an army mental hospital. Daisy had acted too emotionally on her fears about this young man, but the fears were valid. After Daisy contacted the police about Franz, they arrested him and sent him back to Germany.

Amy graduated from the Institut Monte Rosa in 1969, a year ahead of her former classmates back in California. She and her family were ready to return to the United States for Amy's college education. Daisy Tan would discover there, however, that Amy's days of rebelling against her mother's wishes were not over. ✑

# Chapter 5

# AN ADULT NOW

❧❧❧

Back in the United States, Daisy Tan still hoped to keep Amy safe by limiting her educational choices to two Baptist colleges. When Amy enrolled in Linfield College in McMinnville, Oregon, her mother felt relieved. Located in a small town surrounded by farmland, this Baptist college would not expose Amy to the dangers of city life. It also offered the classes that she would need to apply to medical school. Daisy still insisted that her daughter become a doctor.

Yet Daisy could not control the young woman Amy had become or anticipate what would happen when Amy truly fell in love. On a blind date, Amy met Louis M. DeMattei. She and this pre-law student did not expect their date to lead to love, but it did. When Lou moved to California at the end of the school year

*Amy Tan worked on her doctorate in linguistics at the University of California–Berkeley.*

*Lou DeMattei and Amy Tan in 1974*

to continue his education, Amy went with him. Daisy was so angry about the move that she did not speak to Amy for six months.

Amy did keep up her college studies, attending San Jose City College and transferring to San Jose State University. But Amy did not continue with her mother's plans for medical school. Instead of science classes, Amy majored in English and linguistics. She graduated from college in 1973. While she and Lou attended school, they worked in local pizza parlors to support themselves.

Amy continued her academic career at San Jose State University and earned a master's degree in 1974. Her degree was in linguistics, which is the study of the origins and development of language. As she later wrote, "I love the sounds and shapes of words. ... I am fascinated with the origins of words, when they came into being, how they were first used." Amy decided to earn another advanced degree in linguistics. She began classes for a doctorate at the University of California-Santa Cruz and later transferred to the nearby University of California-Berkeley. Amy still planned to be a doctor—a doctor of philosophy in linguistics instead of the medical doctor her parents had wanted.

Amy experienced another milestone in 1974 when she and Lou DeMattei married. While struggling to make ends meet, they became good friends with an engineering major from Wisconsin named Pete. (In her writing, Amy Tan respects the privacy of Pete's family by never mentioning his last name.) Pete worked with the couple on the late shift at a local pizza parlor. The three enjoyed talking about life, dreams, and their hopes. They went backpacking together in Yosemite National Park. To save money, in 1976, Amy, Lou, and Pete shared a two-bedroom apartment.

The apartment mates supported one another emotionally during difficult times at work. Amy was robbed at gunpoint at the pizza parlor. Another time, they had to remove gang members from the store. When these troublemakers sought revenge, they

As Amy Tan grew up, she heard many languages. Her mother spoke broken English, while her father's English was excellent. Tan also heard different Chinese languages. In China, there are different kinds of spoken Chinese. Sometimes, education and location also influence Chinese speech. Daisy Tan spoke upper-class Mandarin and the Chinese used in the city of Shanghai. In the San Francisco area, many Chinese-Americans only spoke Cantonese. Often, they did not understand speakers of Mandarin. Amy sometimes used English to help Daisy and other Chinese-Americans communicate with each other.

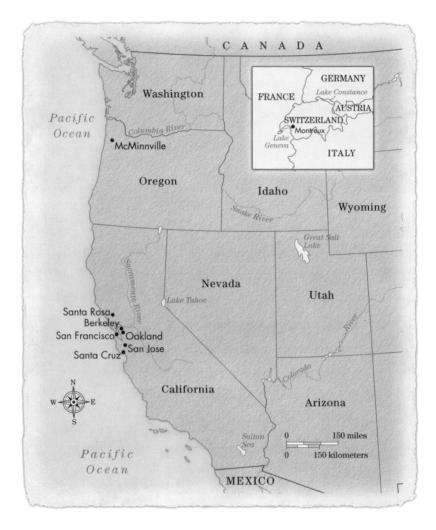

started fistfights and made threats. Pete began to have nightmares about being attacked and killed.

The three young people hoped to solve this problem by moving to the neighboring community of Oakland. On the day before Amy's 24th birthday, she and Lou helped Pete settle into his new apartment there. The couple were on the waiting list for an apartment in the same building. On Amy's birthday, she and Lou left Pete in his new home with a bad cold. Amy did not realize that by the end of her birthday celebration, her ideas about life, dreams, and hopes would be forever changed.

Amy and Lou returned to discover that Pete had been murdered during the night! Thieves had broken in, taken his few valuable belongings, and left Pete tied up in ropes that slowly strangled him. Because his family was in Wisconsin, Amy and Lou had to identify Pete's body for the police. Amy later said that this experience of seeing Pete's face "as it appeared at the moment of death" was "too obscene to relay in words." The effects of this experience lingered. For the next seven years, on the anniversary of Pete's death, Amy would find herself unable to speak for several days.

The murder also had more immediate effects. Pete had died by strangulation, just as he had dreamed. Amy herself now began to dream about Pete. In one dream, he told her the first names of his murderers. The men the police later caught and charged with the crime had the first names Amy had dreamed. In other dreams, Pete urged her to overcome her fears, to fly to new heights. Amy began to wonder if spirits might be real and dreams might be true. Amy did not reach a firm conclusion, later writing of herself, "I am neither a believer nor a skeptic. I am a puzzler." Yet

Pete's murder and Amy's dreams about him led her to make a major change in her life.

Amy wanted to do something useful and worthwhile. Pete had planned to design equipment to help disabled children. He had talked with Amy about her possibly using her language skills to help such children. Now she decided to be brave and fly far from the academic goals of her parents. In 1976, Amy left graduate school before completing her doctorate and began to work with disabled children. For five years, she was a language development specialist for Alameda County. This job gave Amy great satisfaction and also prepared her for later efforts to be a writer. She worked with more than 1,000 families whose children had special needs. Amy later noted that she learned from these families "the limitlessness of hope within the limits of human beings. I learned to have compassion. It was the best training I could have had for becoming a writer."

Yet Amy's first successes as a writer were not the novels that later brought her fame. She started out using her writing talents in business. Amy's interest in helping people was her bridge into the business world, where her first writing job was for a newsletter for other caregivers at a hospital. In 1981, Amy changed careers to become a reporter and later an editor for *Emergency Room Reports*. In 1983, she went into business for herself, writing manuals for

companies such as IBM. She also wrote speeches for executives in companies such as Apple Computers, AT&T, and Pacific Bell.

During this time, Amy and Lou, now a tax attorney, lived in San Francisco. They shared their older home with a Siamese cat named Sagwa. Very successful and busy, Amy did not even think about changing the direction of her life until 1985. That was when Daisy Tan, always important to her daughter, terrified Amy by suddenly becoming ill.

*Amy Tan, who has played the piano since childhood, serenaded her husband, Lou DeMattei.*

# 6 BECOMING A WRITER

*Chapter*

❧❀❧

In early 1985, when Amy and Lou were on vacation in Hawaii, a terrifying message reached them. Four days before, Daisy Tan had apparently suffered a heart attack. She was in the hospital. Daisy might already be dead. As Amy tried frantically to phone the hospital, she vowed never to take her mother for granted again. Daisy had once asked what Amy would remember about her after her death. Amy's vague answer had caused Daisy to say sadly and angrily, "I think you know little percent of me." Amy now promised God and herself that if Daisy survived she would learn her mother's stories. She would travel with her back to China, too.

A relieved Amy was soon speaking to Daisy. Her chest pain, it turned out, had not been a heart attack after all. Daisy had just gotten too excited while arguing with some shopkeepers. She was already well enough to complain about them to her daughter. Yet Amy did not forget the vows she had made.

*Like Tan, Maxine Hong Kingston also writes in personal ways about Chinese immigrants to America and the family life of Chinese-Americans. Her first book,* The Woman Warrior: Memoirs of a Girlhood Among Ghosts, *was published in 1976.*

Her desire to learn more about her mother combined with Amy's recent unhappiness with her career. She was successful writing for large companies, but she worked long hours and was less and less satisfied. Amy earned a lot of money, but she described her work as "meaningless." She had spoken to a doctor about her feelings. She had tried taking jazz piano lessons to see if her childhood piano playing could become a rewarding adult hobby. These efforts did not help. Amy now decided to take up fiction writing—and, in keeping with her vow, she decided to write about her mother's life and her own.

In part, Amy also felt inspired by novels and stories she had begun reading. She appreciated newer writers such as Maxine Hong Kingston, Isabel Allende, and Louise Erdrich, who wrote about ethnic experiences.

Erdrich had recently written

a collection of related stories called *Love Medicine.* These very personal tales about generations within one Native American family moved Tan more than literature she had read as an undergraduate. She later told an interviewer that this book gave her the idea to "write a number of stories linked by community." First, though, she had to sharpen her writing skills.

Tan applied to a selective workshop for beginning writers—the Squaw Valley Community of Writers Workshop. There award-winning writer Molly Giles helped Tan shape a story she had already begun. An article in *Life* magazine about young Chinese-Americans playing the difficult game of chess had prompted this story. As Tan rewrote her story, titled "Endgame," she realized it was more about the relationship between the girl prodigy and her mother than it was about chess. Tan had found a way to write fiction that touched upon her own life. During this workshop, Tan also made friends and contacts who helped her new writing career.

> *Amy Tan knows that the question, "What are you going to become?" sometimes overwhelms kids. She hopes they will remember that she was 35 before she found her "purpose in life—writing fiction." She still had to practice skills to reach this goal.*
>
> *Tan also hopes young people realize that "the essential part of who you are shouldn't always be measured by what others think." She tells them, "Writing and music and anything that allows you to express yourself leads to your finding a friend within yourself—enables a kid to feel a little less lonely."*

Molly Giles sent "Endgame" to the small literary magazine *FM Five*, which published it. The editors of popular *Seventeen* magazine saw the story there. They thought their teenage readers would enjoy Tan's story, so they reprinted it in their November 1986 issue, calling it "Rules of the Game." This tale of young Waverly Jong, her two brothers, and the proud mother who pushes her prodigy daughter too hard next caught the eye of literary agent Sandra Dijkstra. After reading three stories by Tan, she urged Amy to outline enough stories to complete a book. Dijkstra believed that with this outline and the three finished stories, she could convince a major publishing company to buy and publish Tan's book.

Tan excitedly outlined the short stories. They focused on four Chinese women who immigrate to California around 1949 and their complicated relationships with their American-born daughters. One of these mother-daughter pairs is the Jongs from "Rules of the Game." The mothers meet each week to play mah-jongg and jokingly name their group The Joy Luck Club. Each week, their gatherings bring them what is sometimes their only joy and also the chance for good luck at mah-jongg. The older women tell some of Tan's stories, while their daughters tell others.

At first, Tan called her proposed book *Wind and Water*, a reference to feng shui. But Dijkstra thought that the title of one of the outlined stories, "The Joy

Luck Club," would make a better title for the collection overall. Tan agreed. It was *The Joy Luck Club* that Tan thought about as she and Lou got ready, in October 1987, to keep her vow to visit China with Daisy.

Tan's mother had already made one trip back to China by herself in 1978. She had found and joyfully visited the daughters she had left nearly 30 years before. But China remained distant and mysterious to Amy. She worried about meeting her half sisters and felt nervous about this trip.

Her fears proved needless when she met them. As she later said, "There was an instant bond [with my sisters]. The way they smiled, the way they

*Peppers dried by a house as terraced rice fields covered the Chinese landscape.*

Between 1949 and 1972, the relationship between communist China and the democratic United States was strained. There were no official diplomatic relations, trade, or approved tourist visits between these countries. In 1972, President Richard M. Nixon visited China. He and Chinese leaders signed an agreement that opened some trade between their countries. Improved relations had actually begun the previous year when China unexpectedly invited the American table tennis team to visit China. The pingpong players were the first Americans allowed in the country since 1949. What followed became known as "pingpong diplomacy," which resulted in Nixon's visit. In 1978–1979, official diplomatic relations and tourism began.

held their hands, all those things connected me. I had family in China. I belonged." Tan was also relieved to see that her mother was sometimes as demanding and complaining with her half sisters as she had been with Amy herself. Daisy's behavior in China helped Amy realize that her mother's difficult personality was due to the hard life she had led rather than to any failures by Tan. This visit also helped her embrace the Chinese-American identity that had made her feel so painfully different as a girl.

After returning from China, Tan received wonderful news. Dijkstra had sold *The Joy Luck Club*. She had even managed to get Tan an unusually large amount of money in advance of publication—$50,000. With this money, Tan would be able to stop writing for businesses and concentrate all her time and attention on completing her book. Even though Tan never stopped thinking of *The Joy Luck Club* as a short-story collection, the publisher wanted to market it as a novel. Tan now had to write links between the stories plus 13 more stories.

Writing *The Joy Luck Club* did not come easily to Tan. For four months, she wrote at her computer from 9 A.M. to 6 P.M. each weekday. To help herself be creative, she began each workday by lighting incense and listening to relaxing music played through headphones. She rewrote each story between 12 and 20 times. Tan wrote the stories as they came to her, although they would be arranged differently for the book. She would improve her work by reading

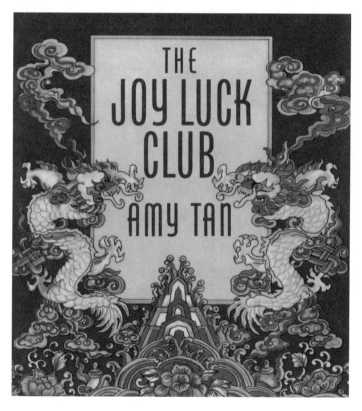

*Amy Tan's first book,* The Joy Luck Club, *was published in 1989 to nearly universal praise.*

The beliefs of the philosopher Confucius (551–479 B.C.) greatly influenced Chinese laws and traditions. Confucius valued order and obedience. He thought men and women had different abilities. The ideal woman, he said, was governed by men. She obeyed her father before marriage, her husband after marriage, and—if a widow—her son. Her four most important virtues were modest behavior, modest speech, pleasing male relatives, and caring for her home. These views affected generations of Chinese women, including Daisy.

it aloud from pages printed from her computer. She later confessed that this method was not good for the ecology: "I figured out that I went through 7,000 sheets of paper writing *The Joy Luck Club.*"

There are many parallels between Amy's and Daisy's experiences and the characters and events in this book. These connections are clear from the very first page of the book, which Tan dedicated to her family with these words:

> To my mother
> and the memory of her mother
> You asked me once
> what I would remember.
> This, and much more.

The strength of each mother and the combination of love and pain that fills each intense mother-daughter relationship are like Daisy and Amy. When the character Suyuan Woo argues with her beloved daughter, she is likely voicing an opinion Tan heard many times from Daisy. Suyuan shouts, "Only two kinds of daughters ... those who are obedient and those who follow their own mind! Only one kind of daughter can live in this house. Obedient daughter!" Her daughter's angry reply echoes the bitter words Amy herself came to regret saying to Daisy.

Yet there is also gentle humor and appreciation in the book, as Tan shows the misunderstandings immigrants experience because of culture differences and their limited English. In an essay, Tan later described how Daisy's imperfect English, which embarrassed Amy as a teenager, was nonetheless Amy's heartfelt "mother tongue," the "vivid, direct ... language that helped shape the way I saw things, expressed things, made sense of the world." With *The Joy Luck Club*, Tan kept her vow to learn and understand more about her mother.

The book is not, however, just a retelling of facts—a biography or autobiography. While Daisy Tan did play mah-jongg weekly with the same

*The Chinese game of mah-jongg has been popular in the United States since the 1920s. To play, four people take turns trying to get winning combinations of different tiles. There are 144 tiles, and each tile is decorated with one of 34 patterns.*

friends, many of the book's details—such as living in San Francisco's Chinatown—were not part of Tan's own life. As Tan has explained, her writing contains "an emotional truth. … What I draw from is not a photographic memory, but an emotional one. When I place that memory of feeling within [fiction] it becomes imagination. Anything can happen." When *The Joy Luck Club* appeared in print in 1989, its "emotional truth" appealed to enormous numbers of readers.

Reviewers praised *The Joy Luck Club*. One newspaper reviewer declared, "The only negative thing I could ever say about this book is that I'll never be able to read it again for the first time." Another literary expert declared that its powerful storytelling described the experiences of all immigrant families, not just Chinese-Americans. In addition to its inclusion on the American Library Association Best Books for Young Adults list, Tan's work won a Bay Area Book Reviewers prize and a Commonwealth Club gold award. It was nominated for the *Los Angeles Times* Best Book of the Year and the National Book Critics Circle's Best Novel. *The Joy Luck Club* was also a finalist for the highly respected yearly National Book Award.

Tan received positive responses from her family as well. When a reporter asked her how Daisy liked the book, Tan said, "She's busy going to bookstores to see if they have the book. If they don't, she scolds them." Tan also received a letter from her half sister,

*Amy Tan (right) shopped at a San Francisco market during the early years of her success.*

Tina Eng. Called Jindo by her family, this sister and her husband had immigrated to the United States and settled in Wisconsin in the 1980s. Jindo wrote admiringly of Tan's achievement, saying that she herself had wanted to write stories.

In the next years, Tan held on to the praise and money that this immensely successful book brought her. In addition to the original sale, Ivy Books paid $1.2 million for the right to print the paperback version. Tan needed to keep all these benefits in mind as she discovered the many problems also involved with being a famous author. &

# 7 A Writer's Life

*Chapter*

⋞⟩✦⟨⋟

As a business writer, Tan had learned the value of publicity. Even before *The Joy Luck Club* appeared in print, she was eager to tell people about her book. Tan made a videotape showing her, Daisy, and Lou walking in San Francisco's colorful Chinatown and attending a mah-jongg game at a real club meeting. When her publisher saw how well Tan communicated on this tape, the company set up numerous radio and television interviews for her. One morning in May 1989, Tan even appeared on the national *Today* show.

Tan was also happy to do more interviews, sign books, and give talks around the country. Her name was becoming familiar to many people, including those who did not often read many novels.

Parts of *The Joy Luck Club* were printed in two

*Amy Tan became a household name after publication of*
The Joy Luck Club.

**61** ✦

widely distributed magazines, the *Atlantic Monthly* and *Ladies' Home Journal.* These excerpts made readers eager to read the entire book and further increased Tan's fame. As *The Joy Luck Club* won awards and was nominated for others, her reputation grew. Tan and her family were thrilled by this success.

Then Tan began to experience the downside of fame. Curious fans who learned her San Francisco address stopped and stared into the windows of her ground-floor home, disturbing Tan's work and making her feel uneasy. Tan and her husband moved from their longtime home to the third floor of a larger building. They also changed their phone number in an effort to live a more private life.

*Amy Tan and Lou DeMattei in her study at their San Francisco home*

Tan learned that fame spread not only the facts of her life but also inaccurate information. She read that her long-ago boyfriend Franz had been "an older German man, who had close contacts … with organized crime." This description did not fit the casual young man involved in small-time illegal activities whom Tan had briefly dated. Tan even read that she had had several husbands. She heard opinions about her next book, but she had not even written it yet. This last bit of misinformation was particularly painful, because Tan was now struggling to start that new book.

Because *The Joy Luck Club* had been so successful, Tan feared that her next work could disappoint people. She met many writers who told her that second books often failed to live up to first ones. Tan became so nervous that she developed hives. Sitting tensely at her desk, she also developed neck and jaw pain, leading her to clench her teeth together. This constant clenching resulted in two cracked teeth and a big dentist's bill. One way to reduce her tension, Tan realized, was to stop giving talks and interviews about *The Joy Luck Club*. She would then have more time and energy for a new project.

Yet Tan had trouble settling on a second project. She started six different books. All dealt in some way with her Chinese heritage, now a source of pride and affection as well as success. As Amy later recalled:

*[I finished] eighty-eight pages of a book about the daughter of a scholar in China who accidentally kills a magistrate. ... I wrote fifty-six pages of a book about a Chinese girl orphaned during the San Francisco earthquake of 1906. I wrote ninety-five pages about a girl who lives in northeast China during the 1930s with her missionary parents. ... I wrote thirty pages about a woman disguised as a man ... [in] San Francisco's Chinatown at the turn of the twentieth century.*

Tan calculated that she wrote close to 1,000 pages before she abandoned these efforts. She realized that one of her problems was thinking about what reviewers and readers now expected of her. She was writing to please them. Each of her ideas had its own "true seed ... the core of the real book," Tan later said, but none of them produced a book that she felt she just had to write. Tan decided she needed to start writing and keep going until she found that one special story.

Wearing headphones that played the same music over and over, Tan wrote for days. She began by writing about a woman cleaning a house—a messy one, just like Tan's. She would write 30 pages, stop, and then start over again from the beginning. Tan wrote more than 150 pages before she realized that her character had a story to tell—and that this story was about Daisy Tan's unhappy first marriage. This story

*Amy Tan and her mother, Daisy, received letters from relatives in China.*

became Tan's second novel, *The Kitchen God's Wife.*

For this book, Tan researched World War II and China during the 1930s and 1940s and interviewed her mother. Daisy was happy to cooperate. She was tired of people asking her which one of the mothers in *The Joy Luck Club* was really her. Daisy had even told Tan at one point, "Next book, tell my true story." Like *The Joy Luck Club*, however, *The Kitchen God's Wife* is much more than a biography. Tan felt that some of what Daisy told her was too personal to include in the novel. Tan did include events in war-torn China that affected Daisy and the people she knew. Yet, in creating the characters of Winnie Louie and her grown daughter, Pearl, what Tan used most of all was her own imagination. And even though this was a story that inspired her, she still labored over it, rewriting hundreds of pages.

*The Kitchen God's Wife* was published in 1991. It begins and ends with the thoughts of Pearl Louie, a Chinese-American woman close to Tan's age. She and her immigrant mother, Winnie, have always had a loving yet tension-filled relationship. Each woman has kept secrets from the other. Most of the novel is told from Winnie's viewpoint.

Pearl listens as Winnie describes her life, from girlhood through 10 years of a brutal marriage and beyond. As a wife, Winnie suffered much like the nameless wife of the spirit traditionally worshipped as the Kitchen God. When this spirit was alive, he is said to have been a selfish and cruel man. Winnie found the strength to leave her bad marriage, even though it also meant leaving daughters behind in China. After she tells Pearl these secrets,

*In China, parents or go-betweens called matchmakers tradition-ally arranged marriages. Young women did not have much, if any, say about whom they mar-ried. Chinese tradition also permitted men to have more than one wife. A wife's role within the household depended on when her husband married her. First wives had the most power. Second, third, and fourth wives held positions of decreasing importance. These marriage customs influenced the lives of Amy Tan's family members in China and often are important in the fiction she writes.*

Winnie is at last able to give the Kitchen God's Wife a name. Out of renewed love and hope for her American-born daughter, Winnie calls this figure Lady Sorrowfree. She is no longer a nameless victim but will instead be a protective spirit for Pearl and other women. The novel ends with mother and daughter having a better understanding of each other.

This exchange of secrets held back until a daughter is an adult mirrors an actual event in Amy Tan's own life. When Tan was in her 30s, she finally heard the tragic story of Daisy's own mother, Jing-

*The story of Daisy Tan (center), who was photographed at age 8 in China, became the inspiration for Amy Tan's second novel.*

*Amy Tan's grandmother Jing-mei (left) was photographed in 1905 with an unidentified relative. Her photo appears on the cover of* The Bonesetter's Daughter.

mei. This woman, Tan's grandmother, had killed herself because of an unhappy marriage. Nine-year-old Daisy had discovered her body. Knowing this helped Tan better understand her own mother and why Daisy had frequently threatened suicide. It hinted at a family history of depression that Tan would later discover. Jing-mei's history became part of Tan's storytelling in several works.

*The Kitchen God's Wife* became a best seller in the United States and six other countries. It won awards and was translated into 20 languages. Although a few reviewers complained that its important mother-daughter relationship makes this book too similar to *The Joy Luck Club*, most reviewers praised Tan's second novel highly. Tan herself has described *The Kitchen God's Wife* as her favorite work.

With this new success, Tan received even more invitations to speak about her books and ideas. Yet, as she later told some college graduates, Tan knew it would be wrong to be content with this fame. She commented jokingly about how well known she had become, referring to a popular TV show and saying, "I have been a *Jeopardy!* question myself." People, she said, should never stop trying to ask important or difficult questions about life, no matter how famous and successful they become. They should find their own voices and show compassion. Tan followed her own advice in the years after *The Kitchen God's Wife* appeared. That is when she dared to search for her own voice in some very different ways.

*When Amy Tan learned about her grandmother's suicide, she realized that depression was probably an illness within her family. This illness, combined with difficult circumstances such as a very unhappy marriage, often leads to suicide or thoughts of suicide. Tan realized that Daisy also probably suffered from depression and that Tan herself had inherited the disease. In 1993, Amy Tan began taking medication for depression. The medicine relieved her ongoing sadness and did not, as she had feared, interfere with her ability to write. She was able to work and live more happily than before.*

*Chapter*

# 8 PICTURES, MUSIC, ACTION!

❦❧

Amy Tan has written that "the best of fiction" helps us "to see the world freshly." After *The Kitchen God's Wife* was published in 1991, the author provided her fans with a fresh look at the world in several new, sometimes unexpected ways. She wrote her first books for children. She also startled and delighted fans by becoming a member of a part-time rock band. And she helped create a successful movie version of *The Joy Luck Club*.

In the spring of 1992, Amy Tan published her first picture book for young readers, *The Moon Lady*. The book is lushly illustrated by her friend Gretchen Schields, a professional artist with 20 years of experience. Schields drew on her own extensive travel in Asia to illustrate Tan's words with detailed images.

*Amy Tan and horror writer Stephen King performed at a benefit concert as part of the Rock Bottom Remainders.*

The Moon Lady, *Amy Tan's first children's book, has won several awards.*

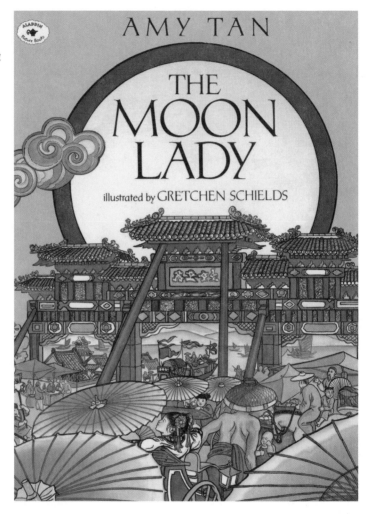

AMY TAN

THE
MOON
LADY

illustrated by GRETCHEN SCHIELDS

*The Moon Lady* is a retelling of the experiences of Ying-ying St. Clair, one of the mothers in *The Joy Luck Club.* In the adult novel, Ying-ying remembers her terrifying experience as a 4-year-old during the traditional autumn Moon Festival. Little Ying-ying misbehaves and falls off her family's boat into deep water. By the time she is rescued and returned to her family, Ying-ying has sadly learned that girls need to be careful and obedient in ways that boys do not. She has learned not to voice what she truly wishes to have—the freedom to play, be herself, and still receive her family's love and approval. Like the Moon Lady of one traditional legend, Ying-ying's wishes have had bad results.

In the picture book, Ying-ying St. Clair is a grandmother, retelling her experiences to her three granddaughters. Now, though, her story teaches about possibilities to explore as well as dangers to be avoided. *The Moon Lady* ends joyfully, with the girls thinking about what they really want and then dancing with their grandmother. Tan said in an interview that she "wanted kids to wonder about wishes: where they come from and who helps us fulfill these wishes throughout our lifetime." She and Gretchen Schields dedicated this hopeful book with love to their nieces.

*The Moon Festival is a harvest holiday celebrated on the 15th day of the eighth month in the Chinese calendar. The moon is brightest on this day, which usually falls in September. There are many legends about the Moon Festival. In one, a selfish wife stole her husband's reward from the gods. She was punished by being sent to live on the moon. Another legend says that the Chinese people overthrew invaders by hiding plans inside small, moon-shaped cakes. During this holiday, family and friends gather to gaze at the moon. They feast on harvest foods and moon cakes.*

In early 1992, Amy Tan explored her own "inner child," by having some of the rock 'n' roll fun her parents denied her as a teen. She joined an amateur rock 'n' roll band whose members are all professional writers. This group jokingly calls itself the Rock Bottom Remainders, a humorous name that refers both to rock music and the low price at which leftover books—called remainders—are often sold in bookstores.

*The Rock Bottom Remainders have been performing since 1992.*

Other members of the Rock Bottom Remainders have included humor writer Dave Barry, cartoonist

Matt Groening, horror writer Stephen King, journalist Mitch Albom, and novelists Scott Turow, Barbara Kingsolver, and Louise Erdrich. None of them are skilled musicians or singers. Amy Tan, a lead singer with the group, cheerfully admits that she cannot sing well. Still, ever since the Remainders' first performance at the 1992 American Booksellers Association convention in California, the band has continued to attract enthusiastic audiences.

People come partly to see their favorite authors acting out in wild and unusual ways. Instead of the elegant long skirts, silk shirts, and soft shawls she usually wears, Tan performs in tiny skirts, halter tops, and thigh-high leather boots. These are appropriate when she belts out what has come to be her special song, "These Boots Are Made for Walking." In one interview, the writer explained, "The rock 'n' roll songs I like the best are the ones with a definite story, often quite stupid stories, like the ones I'll be singing. They're … quite funny to watch." When Tan sings this song, she often pumps up the humor by acting out its tale of an angry, lovesick woman. She treats the other band members scornfully, and playfully pretends to hit them. As she has said, "I don't have a great voice, but the whole song is really about attitude, and I have that. That's basically what our band is about, too. Costumes and attitude."

People also flock to performances because the

Rock Bottom Remainders donate the money from ticket sales to charity. Over the years, the band has contributed more than $300,000 to America Scores, a national organization that helps kids learn to read better. The musician-writers also donate profits from a CD of their music, titled *Stranger Than Fiction*, to PEN, a charity that helps writers around the world.

In 1992, in between band performances, Tan was working on another project, turning *The Joy Luck Club* into a Hollywood movie. This was a thrilling idea for its author, who admits that at one point in childhood, "I thought movies were the ultimate luxury. Perhaps once a month, my parents gave my brothers and me fifty cents each to see a matinee with friends." It was also a scary idea, since she had heard many writers talk about problems transforming books to films.

In 1992, after some delays and disappointments, the movie production began. As one of the movie's producers, Tan had met and approved of Wayne Wang as its director. This Hong Kong-born director said that he wanted to film Chinese-Americans as "real people," unlike the limited roles they typically played in Hollywood movies. Tan had co-written the script with Wang and veteran screenwriter Ron Bass. They had settled on the actors and other crew for the movie. Filming began in the United States and China.

Tan worked hard on this project but also had fun. She pleased the members of Daisy Tan's real-life mah-jongg club by having them appear as extras in the film. Both Daisy and Amy appear briefly in the movie's opening party scene. Tan's niece Melissa has a small speaking part as the daughter of the character Rose. The author was even able to honor the memory of her father and brother Peter by including family photos of them in several scenes.

When the movie version of *The Joy Luck Club* opened on Mother's Day 1993, Daisy Tan was delighted with her daughter's success. She asked a reporter, "What did I do to deserve such a daughter?" Yet Daisy also remarked to Tan that real life was much sadder than anything shown within this film. Tan herself was

*Amy Tan posed with the cast of* The Joy Luck Club *(top row) and members of the real Joy Luck Club.*

very pleased with the movie. She later wrote, "I've now seen the movie about twenty-five times, and I am not ashamed to say that I've been moved to tears each time." Audiences also enjoyed the movie, which grossed more than $32 million.

An event within her own home sparked Amy Tan's next major work, her second picture book for children. Amy and Lou's aging cat Sagwa became very ill. The 17-year-old cat was not expected to live. After dreaming about her pet one night, Tan decided to write about the playful kitten of her memories. Gretchen Schields illustrated the tale, which was published in 1994 as *The Chinese Siamese Cat*. While the book was being written, the real Sagwa made a remarkable recovery. She survived for four more years. Tan has said that it was curiosity that kept her pet alive—Sagwa wanted to see how the story about her turned out.

Tan's two nieces enjoyed reading about Sagwa. These girls, her brother John's daughters, were 3 and 6 years old when Sagwa's story was published. Even though they lived in Canada, Tan kept in close touch with them. She enjoyed having them visit overnight. These connections were especially sweet because Tan and her husband had decided not to have their own children. As she explained in a newspaper interview, she had seen how Daisy suffered when Peter died. Tan recalled her mother saying, "There is

*Since its publication in 1994 as* The Chinese Siamese Cat, *Tan's second children's book has added Sagwa to its title.*

nothing harder than losing a child." Tan admitted that "I would be in fear, constant fear, if I had a child."

In the next years, though, Amy Tan would sadly learn more about the loss of a parent. She would also share with readers the understanding she gained during this difficult time. ✍

*Chapter*

# 9 BETWEEN FAMILY AND FATE

❧❧❧

Family continued to be important in Amy Tan's writing. She now knew and had growing connections with her Chinese half sisters. In 1993, she helped one of them, June Wang (called Lijun by family), immigrate to the United States with her husband and daughter and settle in the San Francisco area. Yuhang Wang, another half sister, remained in Shanghai but visited the United States. The relationship between two half sisters became a main element in Tan's third novel. Titled *The Hundred Secret Senses*, this book appeared in 1995. Its plot alternates between present-day life in the United States and China and 19th-century life in China during the Taiping Rebellion.

The book's main present-day characters are Olivia, an American woman about Tan's own age,

*Chinese rebels stormed a town during the Taiping Rebellion, which plays a part in Amy Tan's third novel,* The Hundred Secret Senses.

and Kwan, her older Chinese half sister. They meet for the first time when Olivia is almost 6 and Kwan, 18, comes to live with Olivia's family. The 19th-century characters are people who Kwan says that she and Olivia were in a past life. According to Kwan, she was then a young Chinese peasant woman and Olivia was an English woman who employed her and became her friend. Kwan knows about past lives and is able to contact the spirit world because she uses abilities most people have but ignore, their "hundred secret senses."

Tan shows the dangers that surround the 19th-century characters. She also describes how Olivia comes to believe in Kwan's vision of their past lives when the sisters travel together to China. This new belief and the trip itself help Olivia transform her life.

Filled with humor and tenderness, as well as adventure, *The Hundred Secret Senses* had a very successful first printing of 550,000 copies. When talking about this book, Tan revealed that some of her ideas had changed. She

*The dust jacket of* The Hundred Secret Senses *featured a smiling Amy Tan. The book received excellent reviews, but not all literary experts and reviewers praise her books. Some say she misleads readers by emphasizing a China that no longer exists. Others say that Tan's writing presents too harsh a view of Chinese men.*

now had a stronger belief in the existence of spirits, in love beyond death, and in fate. As she said, "Everything that happens is neither grand plan nor random coincidence. It is a crazy quilt of love, pieced together, torn apart, repaired again and again, and strong enough to protect us all." This view of life describes not only what happens to the characters in this book but how Tan came to write it.

It seemed to Amy Tan that she was meant to write this novel. She had stumbled upon the hills and caves of its Chinese location while in China filming *The Joy Luck Club*. She was fascinated by this spot and only later learned that it had been important during the Taiping Rebellion. Furthermore, she chose that era in Chinese history for her novel by allowing a book of Chinese history to randomly fall open. While writing the novel, Tan went skiing and injured her leg. The doctor who treated her told her about avalanches, giving her information about the disaster that shapes the life of one of her characters.

> Between 1850 and 1864, a Chinese man named Hung Hsiu-ch'uan led a widespread rebellion against the emperor of China. Christian missionaries had influenced this rebel. He even believed himself to be the younger brother of Jesus. He believed he was meant to lead a new kind of government that would bring taiping, or great peace, to China. He promised that peasants then would own land and women would have greater freedom. Thousands of poor people joined the Taiping Rebellion. They fought many battles with the emperor's army, but the emperor finally defeated the rebels.

*Tan's editor and good friend, Faith Sale, and Daisy Tan on a New York shopping spree*

Discussions, photographs, and even radio music that Tan experienced while writing this novel either echoed its points or gave her new ideas to include.

Still, Tan had trouble finishing *The Hundred Secret Senses*. It still needed 100 pages and was already overdue when she learned that her editor and friend, Faith Sale, had cancer. Tan moved into her friend's New York home to support her during this difficult time. They spent days together, and Tan wrote at night. Although the author later remembered only one night of writing, she completed the novel in the next two months. Perhaps, she later thought, the loving spirits of friends and family guided her in this nighttime project just as loving friendship shaped her days. Daisy Tan had always believed, Amy jokingly remarked, that her daughter's "computer keyboard is a high-tech Ouija board."

In 1995, another illness drew Amy and Daisy even closer. Daisy had begun to forget events and "remember" others that had never taken place. Doctors told Amy that her mother had Alzheimer's disease, which leads over time to total memory loss. Daisy became unable to care for herself. During the next years, Amy and her husband helped Daisy more and more. They made sure that she remained safe and happy. Sometimes, this meant that Amy reassured her mother instead of explaining her mistakes.

Daisy insisted that Amy had been present when Daisy first met her husband John. Amy did not argue with her. She understood that her mother's love for her had placed Amy inside one of Daisy's happiest memories. Sometimes, though, Daisy herself realized her own failing memory. This led to what the author later described as the most healing words her mother ever spoke to her. Late in her illness, Daisy phoned Amy and said:

*I know I did something to hurt you ...
I did terrible things. But now I can't
remember what. ... And I just want to tell
you. ... I hope you can forget, just as I've
forgotten.*

As Amy Tan later wrote, her mother's gifts to her included this knowledge of "what we can forget" as well as what it is important to remember.

During the years of her mother's increasing forgetfulness, Tan continued writing essays and speaking about literature and education. She believes it is important when teaching literature to include authors of all races and backgrounds. Yet she also feels that writers have talents and interests that go beyond their own heritage.

Tan, who considers herself an American writer rather than a Chinese-American one, used her position as a distinguished author to benefit charities in the United States and China. One of these charities helped find homes for Chinese orphans in the United States. In 1996, a British news program about conditions in Chinese orphanages angered the Chinese government. It disliked this bad publicity and decided to limit foreigners' visits to the orphanages. Tan was one of those briefly banned from entering China. She persisted, however, in working for this cause. In 1999, she also completed another major project, selecting and editing a volume of the year's best short stories.

*The Shanghai Children's Home has more than 1,700 orphans in its care.*

Tan had also begun work on a fourth novel. It was based on the life of Daisy's mother, who had been the daughter of a respected traditional healer in China. The manuscript was nearly complete when Daisy Tan entered the last week of her life in 1999. Her entire family gathered around Daisy then. Talking with her sisters, Amy learned her mother's and grandmother's original Chinese names. Tan had not known that these had been changed during hard times.

Within a month of her mother's death, Tan's friend and editor Faith Sale died from cancer. These two deaths convinced Tan that she needed to rewrite her manuscript—to add to it the feelings and ideas that these two losses were stirring within her. As she later explained in an interview, "To find that heart [of the book] and repair the bones, I had to break them into pieces, then start to dig."

*The Bonesetter's Daughter* was published in 2001. Tan chose November 22, the anniversary of her mother's death, for the release date of what she later described as her most personal book. The photograph on its cover is of her own grandmother, Jing-mei, taken when she was 17.

One of this novel's main characters is an older, Chinese-born woman who now has Alzheimer's disease. Part of the book is her autobiography, which tells her story and that of her own mother, the bonesetter's daughter. Both women lived in the area of China where the skeleton of Peking Man was discovered. This archaeological discovery is important in both characters' lives. Another part of the book is told by her grown, Chinese-American daughter named Ruth. She comes to understand "the women who shaped her life, who are in her bones" over the course of the novel. At the book's very end, Ruth also learns her grandmother's original name.

*During the 1920s and 1930s, archaeologists discovered ancient human bones near the city of Beijing, then called Peking. These fossils were between 300,000 and 500,000 years old. Even though they were the remains of women and children as well as men, the fossils came to be known as Peking Man. This discovery excited scientists around the world. Studying Peking Man helped them understand more about the evolution of the human race.*

*The Bonesetter's Daughter* became a best seller. The author completed a four-month-long international book tour to promote her work. But while on this successful tour, Amy Tan began to feel ill. She went to a doctor, expecting quick help. Tan did not know it would be 18 months before her mysterious illness would even be identified.

# 10 MOVING ONWARD

⟨⟩⟨⟩⟨⟩⟨⟩

Chills, headache, extreme tiredness, neck and arm pain, memory loss—these were the first symptoms of Amy Tan's illness. Later, she saw things and people that were not really there. She behaved strangely but did not recall her actions. When doctors could not identify her illness, these symptoms made Tan fear the worst. Perhaps she had inherited a family disease—a brain tumor like her father's or Alzheimer's disease like her mother's. For 18 months, Tan went through medical tests that did not provide definite answers. She even had surgery to remove a growth that doctors found. This did not help.

Tan turned to the Internet, where she found information about Lyme disease. This illness, spread by the bite of certain ticks, in its advanced stages

*Amy Tan's fifth novel,* Saving Fish from Drowning, *was published in 2005.*

causes all of the symptoms Tan had. When Tan was tested and treated for Lyme disease, she finally began to feel better. Yet the disease left her with occasional seizures—sudden, involuntary muscle spasms, sometimes causing unconsciousness. Tan has accepted this painful reality and moved past it. As she notes:

> *The terrorist in my body has been found.*
> *Yes, the world to me is still a scary place*
> *… but I am no longer governed by fear and*
> *fate. I have hope.*

Today, one of the charities Tan supports is LymeAid 4 Kids, which pays medical costs to test sick children for Lyme disease.

Her illness slowed but never totally stopped Amy Tan's professional activities. In 2001, she continued to work and talk about the new television series, *Sagwa the Chinese Siamese Cat.* In 2003, a collection of her essays and speeches titled *The Opposite of Fate: A Book of Musings* appeared in print. In 2005, she completed and published her fifth novel, titled *Saving Fish from Drowning.* Upon its release, eager fans made the novel an immediate best seller.

According to the author, this book grew in part out of a trip she took to Burma. Set mainly in Burma, now sometimes called Myanmar, the book is like Tan's other novels in exploring mother-daughter relationships. It follows the adventures of an American tour group in

Myanmar, whose members include a middle-aged mother and her 12-year-old daughter. Its narrator, Bibi Chen, was a Chinese immigrant to America. Bibi describes her difficult relationship with her stepmother, which affected Bibi throughout her life. Tan has said that this character's voice is like Daisy Tan's.

The book, though, has more main characters than her earlier novels do, and for the first time, the author focuses in depth on the ideas and experiences of male as well as female characters.

A traditional saying sums up the kind of contradictions that Tan's characters face in this novel. Buddhists are not supposed to kill living creatures, so the fishermen of Buddhist Myanmar excuse themselves by saying that they are just "saving fish from drowning." They repeat this saying even though every so-called rescue fails.

*In 1988, a new military leadership took control of the Southeast Asian country of Burma. Leaders renamed their country Myanmar—a name many Burmese people dislike. The government brutally limits the freedom of people there. One famous opponent of Myanmar's government is Burmese leader Aung San Suu Kyi, who won the Nobel Peace Prize in 1991. She is called "The Lady" by the characters in Tan's book. For her beliefs, Suu Kyi has spent more than 10 years under house arrest in Burma. Her activism and continued strength under arrest represent a hope for democracy in Burma.*

Today, Amy Tan remains close with her brother, half sisters, and their families. Lijun, a computer expert, remains in the San Francisco area. Jindo now divides her time between Wisconsin and Shanghai. Yuhang still lives in Shanghai.

Amy Tan continues to live life with zest and humor. She still enjoys hiking and skiing but now is careful to have a companion along in case she has a seizure. She and her husband have homes in San Francisco and New York. Their two tiny dogs are good travelers and keep the author company when she goes on long book tours. Tan also co-owns a prize-winning Yorkshire terrier, and each year she attends the competitive Westminster Dog Show. In 2006, this animal-loving author wrote the foreword to a special book, *Tails of Devotion: A Look at the Bond Between People and Their Pets.* Its sales support five San Francisco charities that rescue and help animals. Tan also continues to perform for charity with the fun-loving Rock Bottom Remainders.

Tan has playfully combined her writing and charitable interests in another way. She has twice auctioned off the right to have the highest bidder's own name used for a character in one of her novels. The auctions were held on the Internet through eBay. To help the fight against lung cancer, Roxanne Scarangello placed the highest bid in the first auction. One of the tourists in *Saving Fish from Drowning* has her name. In September 2005, Tan held another auction to support the First Amendment Project, a group that protects free speech in the United States.

Amy Tan's New York apartment is in the Soho district. She and her husband also have a home in San Francisco.

Forty-seven people placed bids, and the winner paid $3,338.88. Tan will use this person's name in her next novel, which may appear as early as 2007.

Amy Tan's fans eagerly await this book and other works by her. They value her observations about family life, China, being Chinese-American, and life in today's complex world. They appreciate Tan's sharing with readers her personal struggles and triumphs. Fans have come to expect the best writing from this author—fiction and essays that, in her own words, make a connection "between our brain and our heart." ॐ

## TAN'S LIFE

**1952**

Born in Oakland, California

**1967**

Brother Peter dies

**1968**

Father dies; attends private school in Switzerland for a year and graduates from high school there in 1969

**1950**

**1952**

The Walter-McCarran Act allows Japanese immigrants to become naturalized citizens of the United States

**1967**

The first heart transplant is performed by Dr. Christiaan Barnard in South Africa; the surgery is a success, but the patient lives only 18 days

**1969**

U.S. astronauts Neil Armstrong and Edwin "Buzz" Aldrin are the first people to land on the moon

## WORLD EVENTS

## 1974
Earns master's degree; marries Louis M. DeMattei; begins doctoral work in linguistics

## 1970
Begins college in Oregon, later transferring to colleges in San Jose, California, where she graduates in 1973

## 1976
Apartment mate is murdered; leaves graduate school and begins work as a language development specialist with disabled children

## 1975

## 1971
The first microprocessor is produced by Intel

## 1976
U.S. military academies admit women

## TAN'S LIFE

**1989**

*The Joy Luck Club* is published

**1987**

Visits China for the first time

**1991**

*The Kitchen God's Wife* is published

**1990**

**1989**

Chinese troops fire on student pro-democracy demonstrators in Tiananmen Square in Beijing, China, killing an estimated 2,000 or more

**1991**

The Soviet Union collapses and is replaced by the Commonwealth of Independent States

**1987**

Stock markets fall sharply around the world on Black Monday, October 19

## WORLD EVENTS

## 1992

*The Moon Lady*
is published; first
performs with musical
group the Rock
Bottom Remainders

## 1993

*The Joy Luck Club*
movie debuts

## 1994

*The Chinese Siamese
Cat* is published

### 1995

## 1994

Genocide of 500,000
to 1 million of the
minority Tutsi group
by rival Hutu people
in Rwanda

## 1993

The former
Czechoslovakia
divides into the
independent Slovakia
and Czech Republic

## TAN'S LIFE

### 1995

*The Hundred Secret Senses* is published; mother Daisy is diagnosed with Alzheimer's disease

### 1999

Selects and edits a collection of the year's best short stories; mother dies

### 2001

*The Bonesetter's Daughter* is published; *Sagwa the Chinese Siamese Cat* television show debuts; symptoms of advanced Lyme disease appear

## 2000

### 1995

Astronaut Eileen Collins becomes the first woman to pilot a U.S. space shuttle

### 1999

King Hussein of Jordan and King Hassan II of Morocco die

### 2001

Terrorist attacks on the two World Trade Center Towers in New York City and on the Pentagon in Washington, D.C., leave thousands dead

## WORLD EVENTS

**2003**

*The Opposite of Fate: A Book of Musings* is published

**2005**

*Saving Fish from Drowning* is published

**2006**

Joins the *Los Angeles Times* as literary editor of the paper's Sunday magazine; writes foreword to *Tails of Devotion*

## 2005

**2003**

Heat wave scorches Europe; more than 35,000 people die

**2005**

Major earthquake kills thousands in Pakistan

**2006**

Within a day of each other, two women become the first female presidents of their countries—Ellen Johnson-Sirleaf in Liberia and Michelle Bachelet in Chile

**DATE OF BIRTH:** February 19, 1952

**CHINESE NAME:** An-Mei
("blessing from America")

**BIRTHPLACE:** Oakland, California

**FATHER:** Yuehhan (John) Tan
(1913–1968)

**MOTHER:** Du Ching (Daisy) Tan
(1916–1999)

**EDUCATION:** Bachelor's and master's
degrees from San Jose
State University; doctoral
degree classes at the
University of California–
Santa Cruz and the
University of California–
Berkeley

**SPOUSE:** Louis M. DeMattei
(September 15, 1950– )

**DATE OF MARRIAGE:** 1974

**SIBLINGS:** Half sister Yuhang Wang
(1936– )
Half sister Tina (Jindo)
Eng (1942– )
Half sister June (Lijun)
Wang (1944– )
Half brother who died at
age 2 or 3
Brother Peter (1950–
1967)
Brother John (1954– )

## Further Reading

Bloom, Barbara Lee. *The Chinese Americans.* San Diego: Lucent Books, 2002.

Tan, Amy. *The Chinese Siamese Cat.* New York: Macmillan, 1994.

Tan, Amy. *The Joy Luck Club.* New York: G.P. Putnam's Sons, 1989.

Tan, Amy. *The Hundred Secret Senses.* New York: G.P. Putnam's Sons, 1995.

Tan, Amy. *The Opposite of Fate: A Book of Musings.* New York: G.P. Putnam's Sons, 2003.

## Look for more Signature Lives

### BOOKS ABOUT THIS ERA:

Amelia Earhart: *Legendary Aviator*
ISBN 0-7565-1880-6

Thomas Alva Edison: *Great American Inventor*
ISBN 0-7565-1884-9

Langston Hughes: *The Voice of Harlem*
ISBN 0-7565-0993-9

Wilma Mankiller: *Chief of the Cherokee Nation*
ISBN 0-7565-1600-5

J. Pierpont Morgan: *Industrialist and Financier*
ISBN 0-7565-1890-3

Eleanor Roosevelt: *First Lady of the World*
ISBN 0-7565-0992-0

Franklin Delano Roosevelt: *The New Deal President*
ISBN 0-7565-1586-6

Elizabeth Cady Stanton: *Social Reformer*
ISBN 0-7565-0990-4

Gloria Steinem: *Champion of Women's Rights*
ISBN 0-7565-1587-4

Booker T. Washington: *Innovative Educator*
ISBN 0-7565-1881-4

## On the Web

For more information on *Amy Tan*, use FactHound.

1. Go to *www.facthound.com*
2. Type in this book ID: 0756518768
3. Click on the *Fetch It* button.

FactHound will find the best Web sites for you.

## Historic Sites

Museum of Chinese in the Americas (MoCA)
70 Mulberry St.
New York, NY 10013
212/619-4785
Museum about the history and culture of the Chinese and their descendants in the Western Hemisphere

Chinese American Museum
425 N. Los Angeles St.
Los Angeles, CA 90012
213/485-8567
Museum about the Chinese-Americans in California

**coincidence**
something that happens accidentally at the same time as something else

**communist**
a supporter of an economic system in which property is owned by the government or community and profits are shared

**compassion**
sadness for someone in trouble that leads to the desire to help that person

**heritage**
the culture and traditions of one's family, ancestors, or country

**investing**
putting money into a project or business hoping to get more money back

**magistrate**
a minor government official with specific, limited power, such as a judge

**musings**
quiet thoughts, which often examine a person's beliefs or experiences

**nominated**
named someone as a candidate for an award, job, or government position

**prodigy**
someone who at a young age is extraordinarily good at an activity

**rebellion**
an armed revolt against a government

**skeptic**
someone who doubts or questions beliefs

## Chapter 1

Page 10, line 8: Amy Tan. *The Chinese Siamese Cat.* New York: Macmillan, 1994, unpaginated, p. 12.

Page 11, line 2: Gerrye Wong. "Bringing Her Cat Tale to Life." *Asian Week Archives.* 11 Oct. 2005, www.asianweek.com/2000_12_22/ae3_amytanreadscattale.html

Page 11, line 16: Sau-Ling Cynthia Wong. "Sugar Sisterhood: Situating the Amy Tan Phenomenon." *The Ethnic Canon: Histories, Institutions, and Interventions.* Ed. David Palumbo-Liu. Minneapolis: University of Minnesota Press, 1995, p. 175.

## Chapter 2

Page 15, line 6: Mary Ellen Snodgrass. *Amy Tan: A Literary Companion.* Jefferson, N.C.: McFarland, 2004, p. 8.

Page 18, line 10: Amy Tan. *The Opposite of Fate: A Book of Musings.* New York: G.P. Putnam's Sons, 2003, p. 17.

Page 19, line 3: Ibid., p. 18.

Page 19, line 15: Ibid., p. 79.

Page 20, line 16: Ibid., p. 136.

Page 20, line 24: Ibid., p. 135.

Page 22, line 18: Ibid., p. 209.

Page 23, line 10: Ibid., p. 111.

## Chapter 3

Page 26, line 3: Ibid., p. 22.

Page 26, line 13: Ibid., p. 137.

Page 27, line 3: Ibid.

Page 28, line 18: Ibid., p. 215.

Page 29, line 9: Ibid., p. 125.

Page 30, line 6: Ibid., p. 126.

Page 30, line 18: Ibid., p. 127.

Page 31, line 18: Ibid., p. 369.

## Chapter 4

Page 33, lines 5, 8: Ibid., p. 24.

Page 33, line 14: Ibid., p. 11.

Page 34, line 12: Ibid., p. 26.

Page 35, line 12: Ibid., p. 27.

Page 37, line 17: Ibid., p. 30.

Page 37, line 28: Ibid., p. 218.

Page 38, line 7: Ibid., p. 213.

Page 39, line 5: Ibid.

## Chapter 5

Page 42, line 23: Ibid., pp. 221–222.

Page 45, line 12: Ibid., p. 49.

Page 45, line 27: Ibid., p. 59.

Page 46, line 16: Ibid., p. 56.

## Chapter 6

Page 49, line 10: Ibid., p. 357.

Page 50, line 10: Ibid., p. 343.

Page 51, line 8: *Amy Tan: A Literary Companion*, p. 15.

Page 51, sidebar: Amy Tan. Phone interview. 4 Jan. 2006.

Page 53, line 12: Barbara Kramer. *Amy Tan: Author of The Joy Luck Club*. Springfield, N.J.: Enslow Publishers, 1996, p. 44.

Page 56, line 4: Ibid., p. 49.

Page 56, line 14: Amy Tan, *The Joy Luck Club*. New York: G.P. Putnam's Sons, 1989, unpaginated, p. 7.

Page 56, line 25: Ibid., p. 142.

Page 57, line 10: *The Opposite of Fate: A Book of Musings*, p. 273.

Page 58, line 4: Ibid., p. 109.

Page 58, line 11: *Amy Tan: Author of The Joy Luck Club*, p. 56.

Page 58, line 26: Ibid., p. 60.

## Chapter 7

Page 63, line 3: *The Opposite of Fate: A Book of Musings*, p. 9.

Page 64, line 1: Ibid., pp. 329–330.

Page 64, line 18: Ibid., p. 330.

Page 65, line 7: *Amy Tan: Author of The Joy Luck Club*, p. 67.

Page 69, line 18: *The Opposite of Fate: A Book of Musings*, p. 293.

## Chapter 8

Page 71, lines 1, 2: Ibid., p. 354.

Page 73, line 24: Ibid., p. 82.

Page 75, line 17: Sharon Wootton. "Novel Musicians." Herald.Net. Snohomish County's Online News Source. 28 Sept. 2005. www.heraldnet.com/ae/story.cfm?sectionname=MUSIC&file=03041816810444.cfm

Page 75, line 24: Teresa Weaver. "Stranger than Fiction." *Atlanta Journal-Constitution*. 28 Sept. 2005. www.rockbottomremainders.com/Atlanta_journal.htm

Page 76, line 12: *The Opposite of Fate: A Book of Musings*, p. 177.

Page 76, line 21: *Amy Tan: A Literary Companion*, p. 21.

Page 77, line 11: Ibid.

Page 78, line 1: *The Opposite of Fate: A Book of Musings*, p. 202.

Page 78, line 28: *Amy Tan: Author of The Joy Luck Club*, p. 93.

## Chapter 9

Page 82, line 10: Amy Tan. *The Hundred Secret Senses*. New York: G.P. Putnam's Sons, 1995, p. 212.

Page 83, line 4: *The Opposite of Fate: A Book of Musings*, p. 266.

Page 85, line 8: *Amy Tan: A Literary Companion*, p. 23.

Page 86, line 1: *The Opposite of Fate: A Book of Musings*, pp. 219–220.

Page 86, line 7: Ibid., p. 220.

Page 87, line 15: *Amy Tan: A Literary Companion*, p. 24.

Page 88, line 23: Amy Tan. *The Bonesetter's Daughter*. New York: G.P. Putnam's Sons, 2001, p. 352.

## Chapter 10

Page 92, line 7: *The Opposite of Fate: A Book of Musings*, p. 369.

Page 93, line 23: Amy Tan. *Saving Fish from Drowning*. New York: G.P. Putnam's Sons, 2005, p. 162.

Page 95, line 11: *The Opposite of Fate: A Book of Musings*, p. 339.

"Amy Tan." 25 Oct. 2005. www.amytan.net

Chan, Sucheng. *Asian-Americans: An Interpretive History.* Boston: Twayne, 1991.

Epel, Naomi. *Writers Dreaming* (Interviews). New York: Vintage, 1993.

Hausmann, Renee. *Amy Tan in the Classroom: The Art of Invisible Strength.* Urbana, Ill.: National Council of Teachers of English, 2005.

Huntley, E.D. *Amy Tan: A Critical Companion.* Westport, Conn.: Greenwood Press, 1998.

Ling, Huping. *Surviving on the Gold Mountain: A History of Chinese American Women and Their Lives.* Albany: State University of New York Press, 1998.

Marsh, Dave, ed. *Mid-Life Confidential: The Rock Bottom Remainders Tour America with Three Chords and an Attitude.* New York: Viking, 1994.

Okihiro, Gary Y. *The Columbia Guide to Asian American History.* New York: Columbia University Press, 2001.

Pottruck, Emily Scott. *Tails of Devotion: A Look at the Bond Between People and Their Pets.* Foreword by Amy Tan. San Francisco: Tails of Devotion, 2006.

"The Rock Bottom Remainders." 28 Sept. 2005. www.rockbottomremainders.com/

"The Salon Interview: Amy Tan, The Spirit Within." 9 Feb. 2006. www.salon.com/12nov1995/feature/tan.html.

Snodgrass, Mary Ellen. *Amy Tan: A Literary Companion.* Jefferson, N.C.: McFarland, 2004.

Takaki, Ronald T. *Strangers from a Different Shore: A History of Asian Americans.* Updated and rev. ed. Boston: Little, Brown, 1998.

Tan, Amy. *The Bonesetter's Daughter.* New York: G.P. Putnam's Sons, 2001.

Tan, Amy. *The Chinese Siamese Cat.* New York: Macmillan, 1994.

Tan, Amy. *The Hundred Secret Senses.* New York: G.P. Putnam's Sons, 1995.

Tan, Amy. *The Joy Luck Club.* New York: G.P. Putnam's Sons, 1989.

Tan, Amy. *The Kitchen God's Wife.* New York: G.P. Putnam's Sons, 1991.

Tan, Amy. *The Moon Lady.* New York: Macmillan, 1992.

Tan, Amy. *The Opposite of Fate: A Book of Musings.* New York: G.P. Putnam's Sons, 2003.

Tan, Amy. *Saving Fish from Drowning.* New York: G.P. Putnam's Sons, 2005.

Trickey, Helen. "Rockin' with the Rock Bottom Remainders." CNN.com. 28 Sept. 2005, www.cnn.com/2003/SHOWBIZ/books/05/27/rock.bottom.remainders

Weaver, Teresa. "Stranger than Fiction." Atlanta Journal-Constitution. 28 Sept. 2005, www.rockbottomremainders.com/Atlanta_journal.htm

Wong, Gerrye. "Bringing Her Cat Tale to Life." Asian Week Archives. 22 Dec. 22, 2000–4 Jan. 2001. 11 Oct. 2005, www.asianweek.com/2000_12_22/ae3_amytanreadscattale.html

Wong, Sau-Ling Cynthia. "Sugar Sisterhood: Situating the Amy Tan Phenomenon." *The Ethnic Canon: Histories, Institutions, and Interventions.* Ed. David Palumbo-Liu. Minneapolis: University of Minnesota Press, 1995.

Wootton, Sharon. "Novel Musicians." Herald.Net. Snohomish County's Online News Source. April 18, 2003. 28 Sept. 2005. www.heraldnet.com/ae/story.cfm?sectionname=MUSIC&file=03041816810444.cfm

Yang, Belle. *Baba: A Return to China Upon My Father's Shoulders.* Preface by Amy Tan. New York: Harcourt Brace, 1994.